# What Mom Said
# vs.
# What Dad Heard

by MommyHooray

What Mom Said vs. What Dad Heard
by MommyHooray



Written and published under the pen name MommyHooray.
Illustrations created using digital illustration tools.

Printed in the United States of America.

ISBN: 978-1-972071-57-1



For more stories and updates, visit:
https://sites.google.com/view/mommyhooray

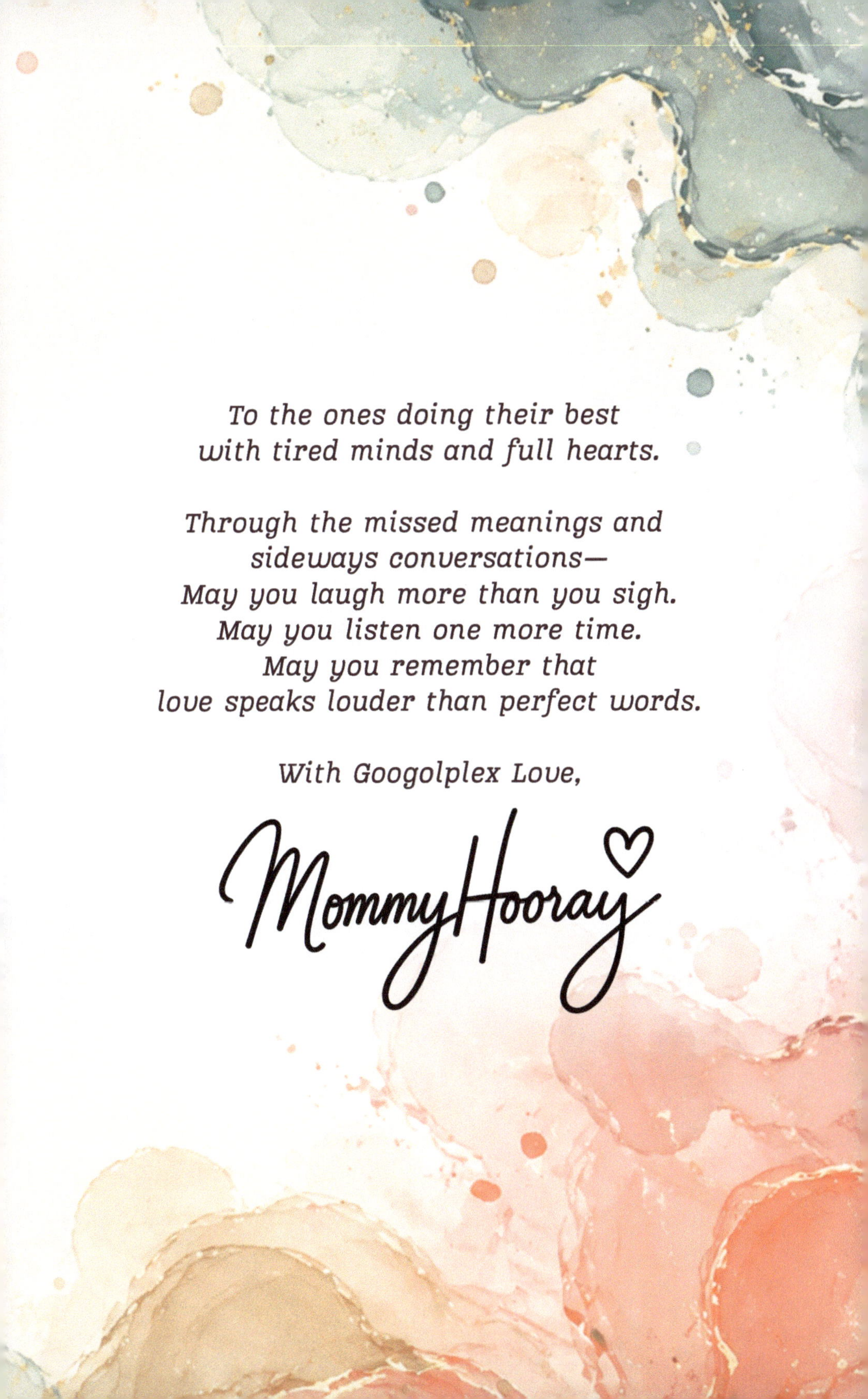

*To the ones doing their best*
*with tired minds and full hearts.*

*Through the missed meanings and*
*sideways conversations—*
*May you laugh more than you sigh.*
*May you listen one more time.*
*May you remember that*
*love speaks louder than perfect words.*

*With Googolplex Love,*

MommyHooray

*The words get messy.*
*The meaning gets lost.*
*But the connection stays.*

In every home, conversations are happening all day long.

Simple ones. Quick ones. The kind that should be easy.

And yet... somehow, they don't always land the way they were meant to.

A sentence goes out one way,
and comes back... slightly rearranged.

Not wrong.
Not right.
Just... different.

This book is about those moments.
The everyday exchanges that take a small detour and turn into something unexpected.

Because between what's said and what's heard, there's a space where imagination, assumption, and real life all collide.

And if you look closely,
that space is usually where the laughter lives.

Let's step into it.

# The Laundry Situation

What Mom said:
*"Can you do the laundry?"*

What Dad heard:
*"Interact briefly with one clothing item."*

What Mom might have meant:
*"Please handle the entire laundry operation from start to finish."*

What Mom said:

*"We just need to make a quick stop."*

What Dad heard:

*"This will take 45 minutes minimum."*

What Mom might have meant:

*"Five minutes. In and out. No wandering."*

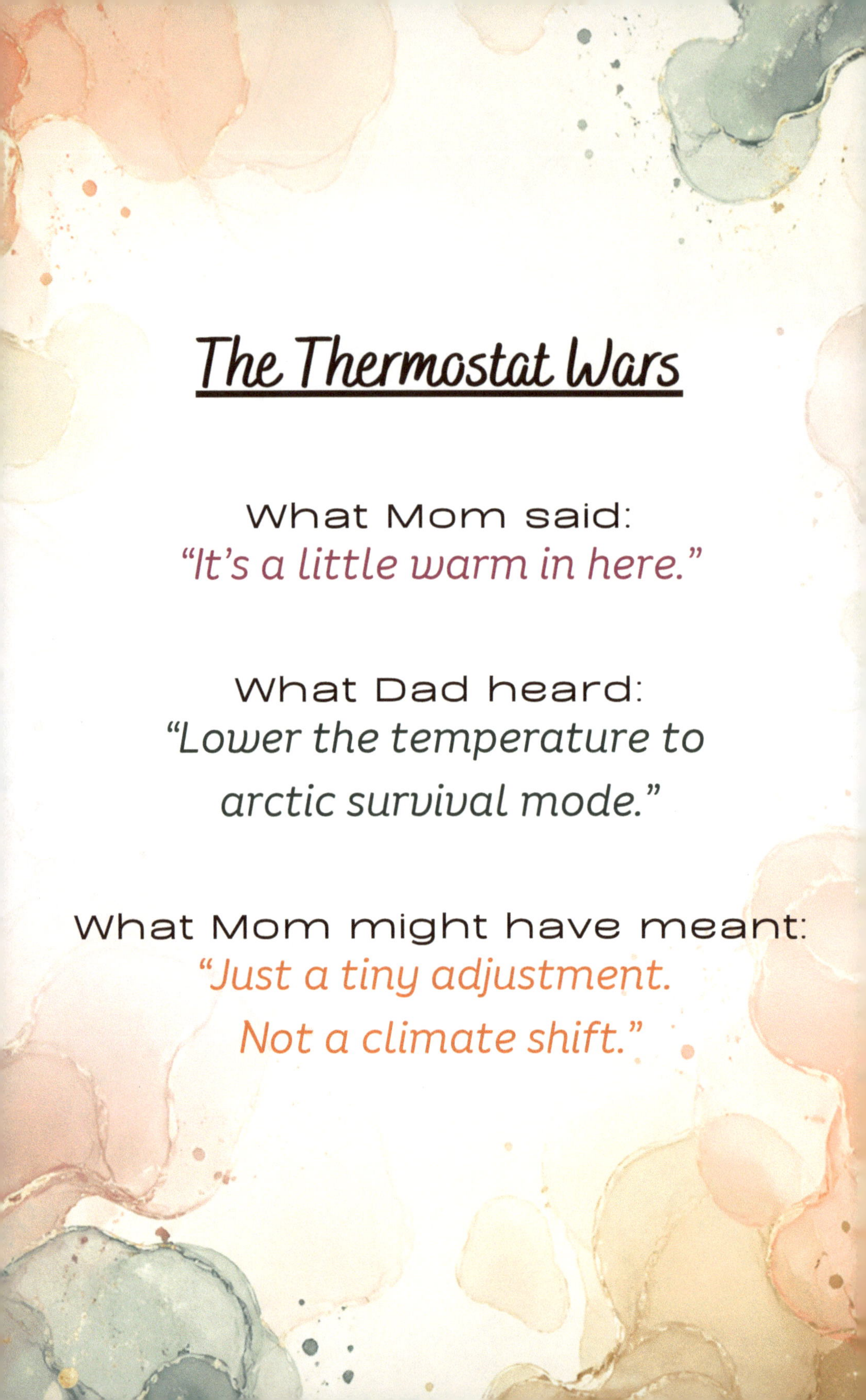

# The Thermostat Wars

What Mom said:

*"It's a little warm in here."*

What Dad heard:

*"Lower the temperature to arctic survival mode."*

What Mom might have meant:

*"Just a tiny adjustment. Not a climate shift."*

# The Grocery Run

What Mom said:
*"We need groceries."*

What Dad heard:
*"Buy snacks!"*

What Mom might have meant:
*"We are out of everything.*
*Please restock our food supply."*

CHIPS
CHOCOLATE
COOKIES
CANDY

# The Toy Situation

What Mom said:
*"Can you clean up the toys?"*

What Dad heard:
*"Relocate one toy*
*and call it progress."*

What Mom might have meant:
*"All. Of. Them."*

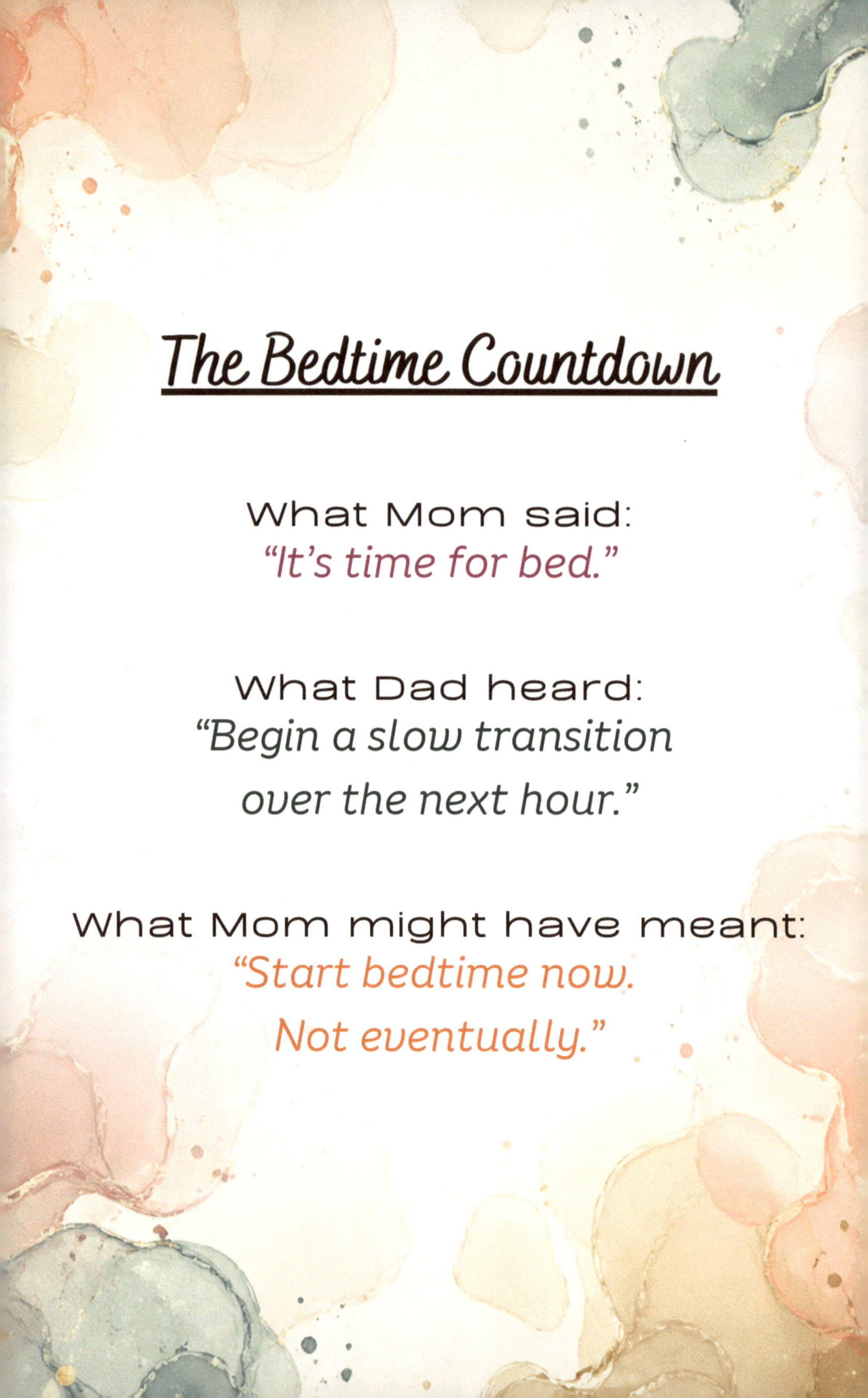

# The Bedtime Countdown

What Mom said:
*"It's time for bed."*

What Dad heard:
*"Begin a slow transition over the next hour."*

What Mom might have meant:
*"Start bedtime now. Not eventually."*

# The Dish Dilemma

What Mom said:
*"Can you do the dishes?"*

What Dad heard:
*"Rinse something."*

What Mom might have meant:
*"Finish the entire sink situation."*

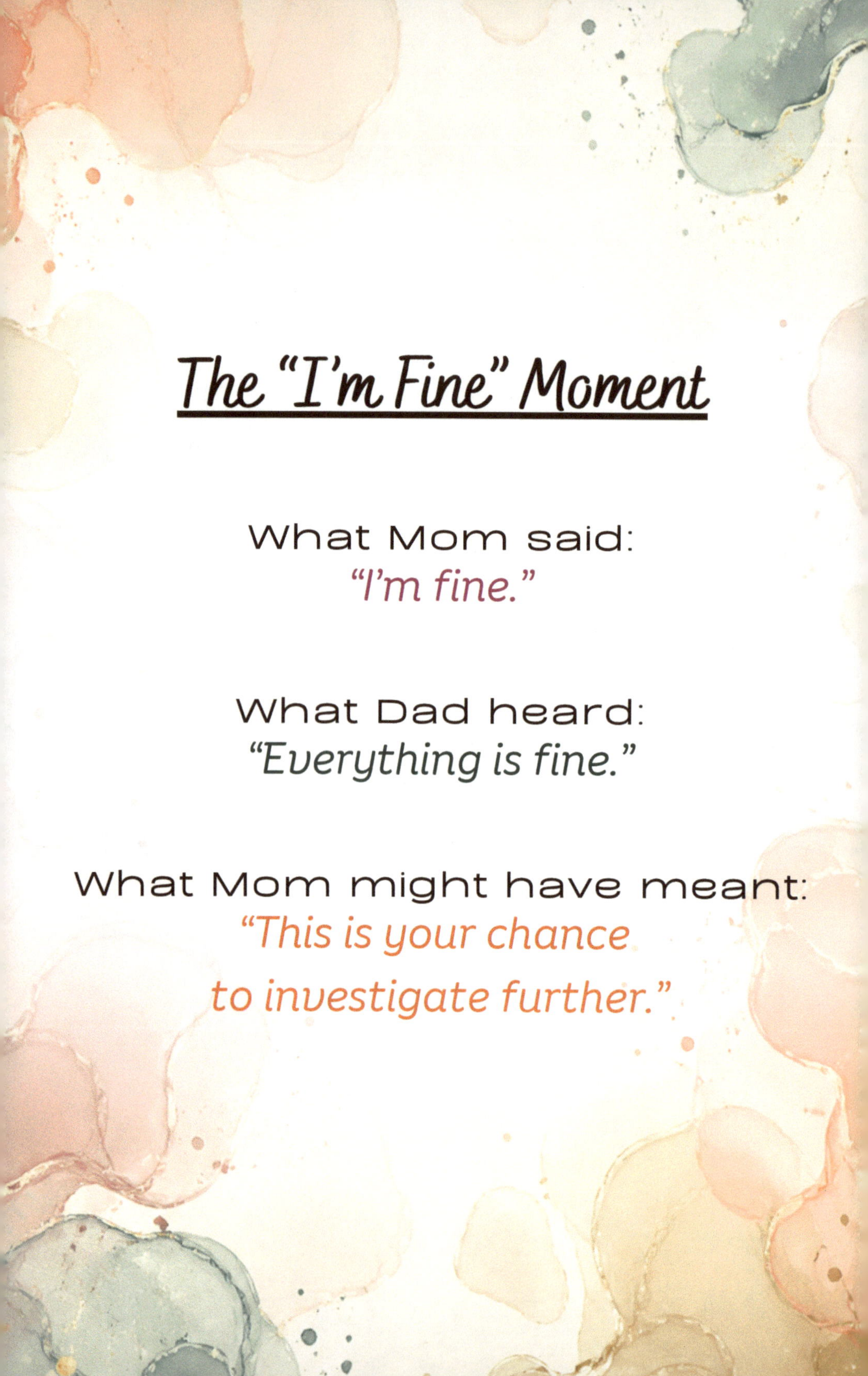

# The "I'm Fine" Moment

What Mom said:
*"I'm fine."*

What Dad heard:
*"Everything is fine."*

What Mom might have meant:
*"This is your chance to investigate further."*

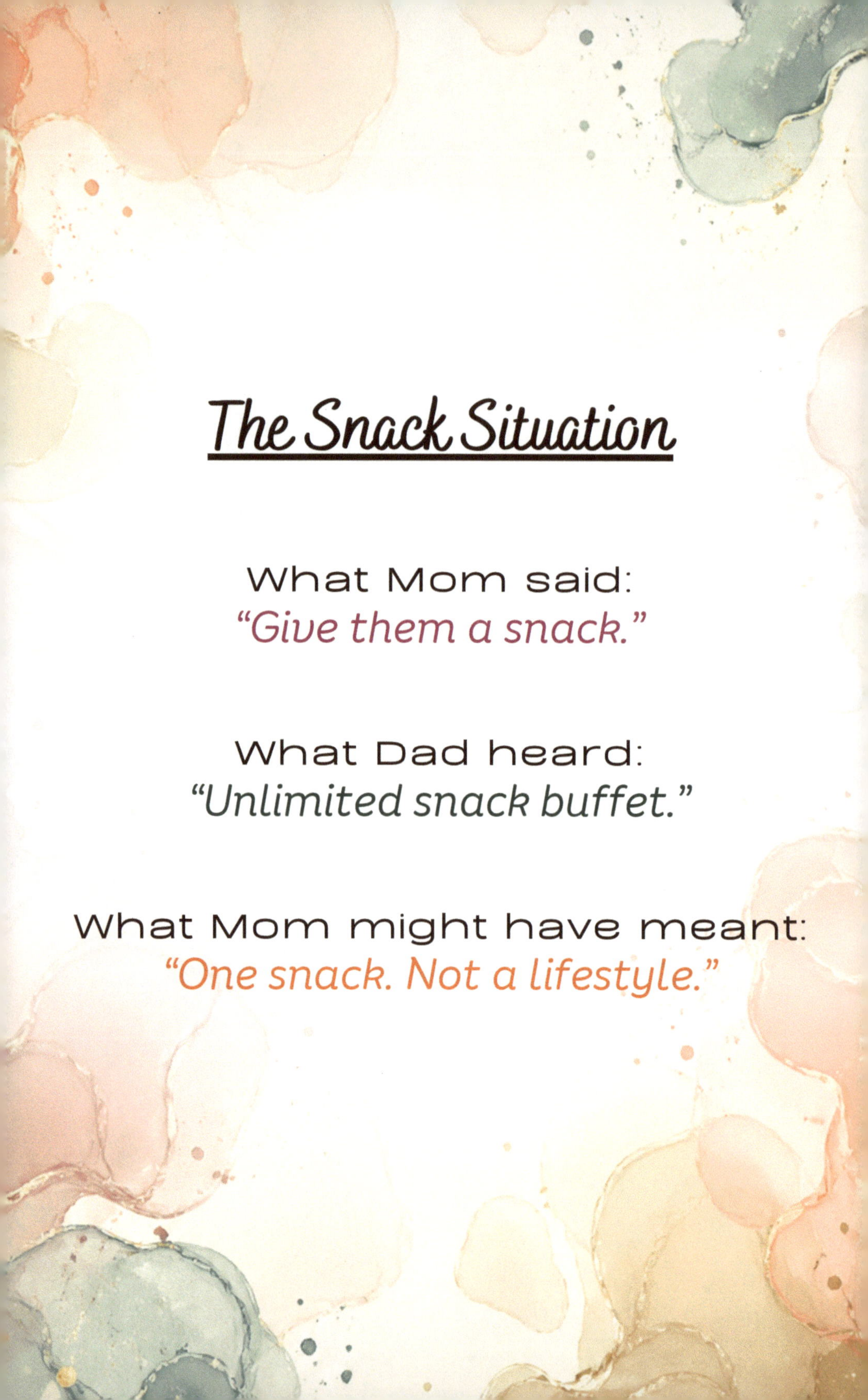

# The Snack Situation

What Mom said:
*"Give them a snack."*

What Dad heard:
*"Unlimited snack buffet."*

What Mom might have meant:
*"One snack. Not a lifestyle."*

What Mom said:
*“Take out the trash.”*

What Dad heard:
*“Stare at it.”*

What Mom might have meant:
*“Now. Please.*
*Before it starts making decisions.”*

Begin
EACH WITH
DAY A
grateful
HEART

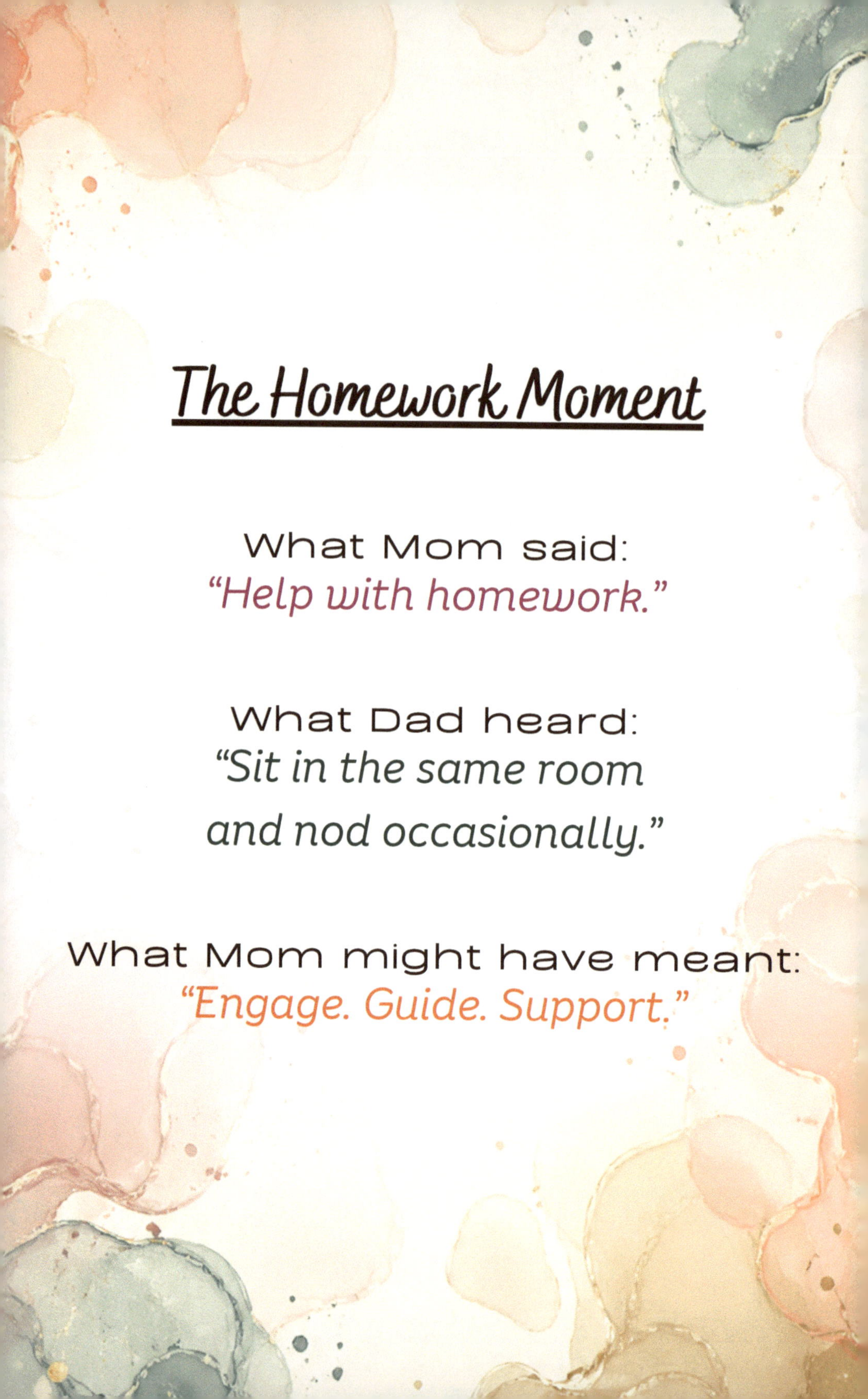

# The Homework Moment

What Mom said:
*"Help with homework."*

What Dad heard:
*"Sit in the same room and nod occasionally."*

What Mom might have meant:
*"Engage. Guide. Support."*

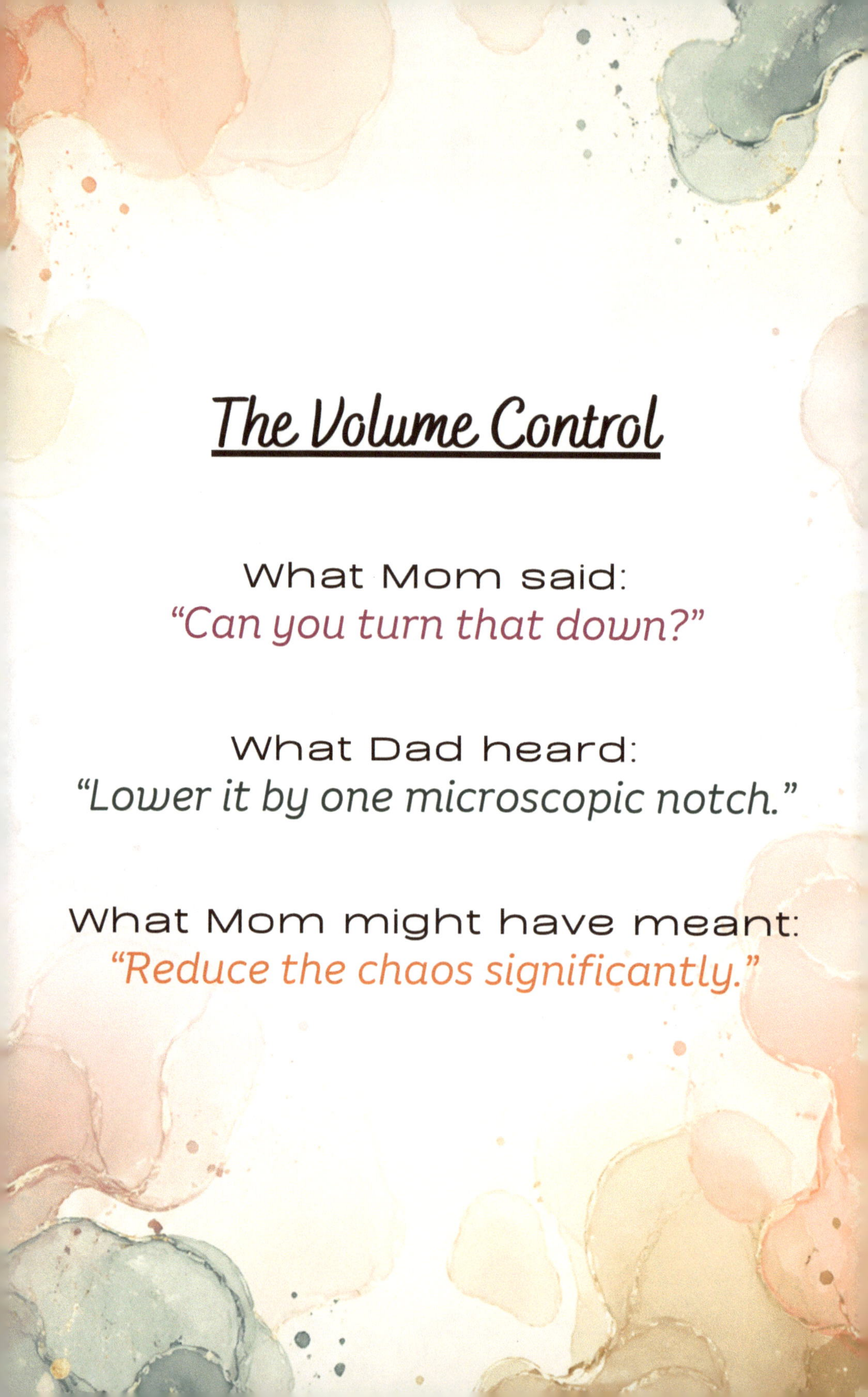

# The Volume Control

What Mom said:
*"Can you turn that down?"*

What Dad heard:
*"Lower it by one microscopic notch."*

What Mom might have meant:
*"Reduce the chaos significantly."*

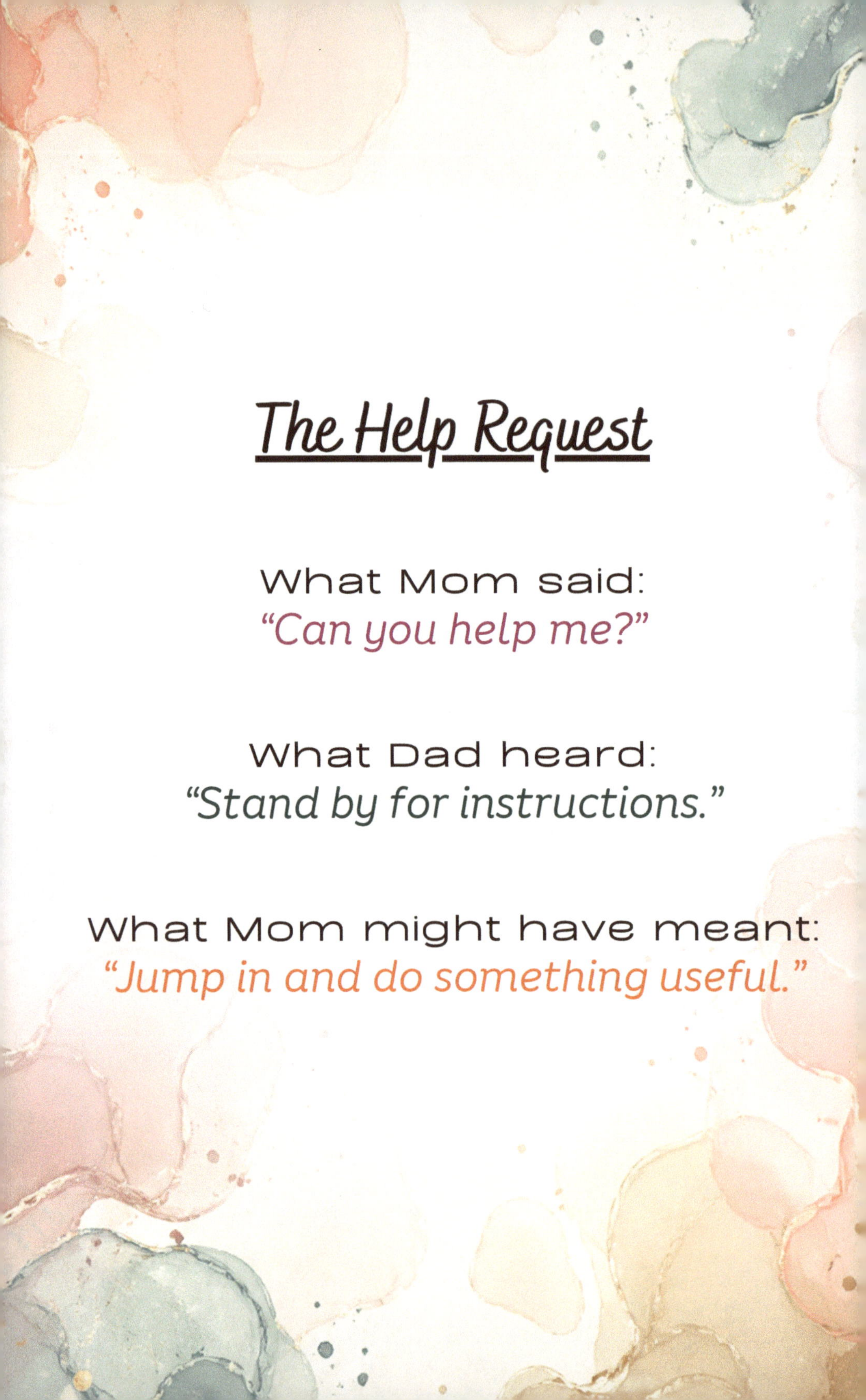

# The Help Request

What Mom said:
*"Can you help me?"*

What Dad heard:
*"Stand by for instructions."*

What Mom might have meant:
*"Jump in and do something useful."*

Trust THE Journey

What Mom said:
*"Watch the kids."*

What Dad heard:
*"Be in the same general area."*

What Mom might have meant:
*"Eyes on them*
*like security cameras."*

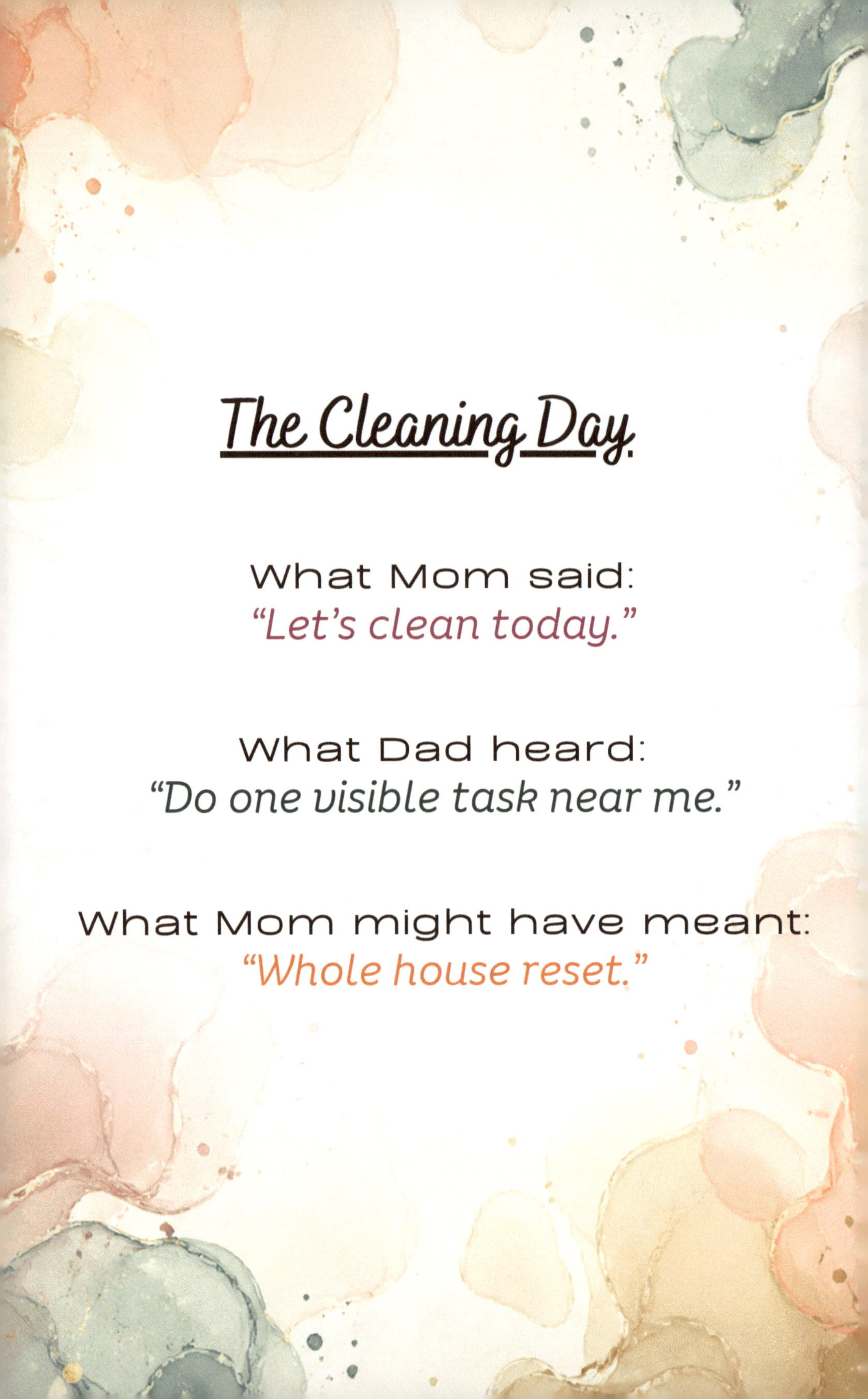

# The Cleaning Day

What Mom said:
*"Let's clean today."*

What Dad heard:
*"Do one visible task near me."*

What Mom might have meant:
*"Whole house reset."*

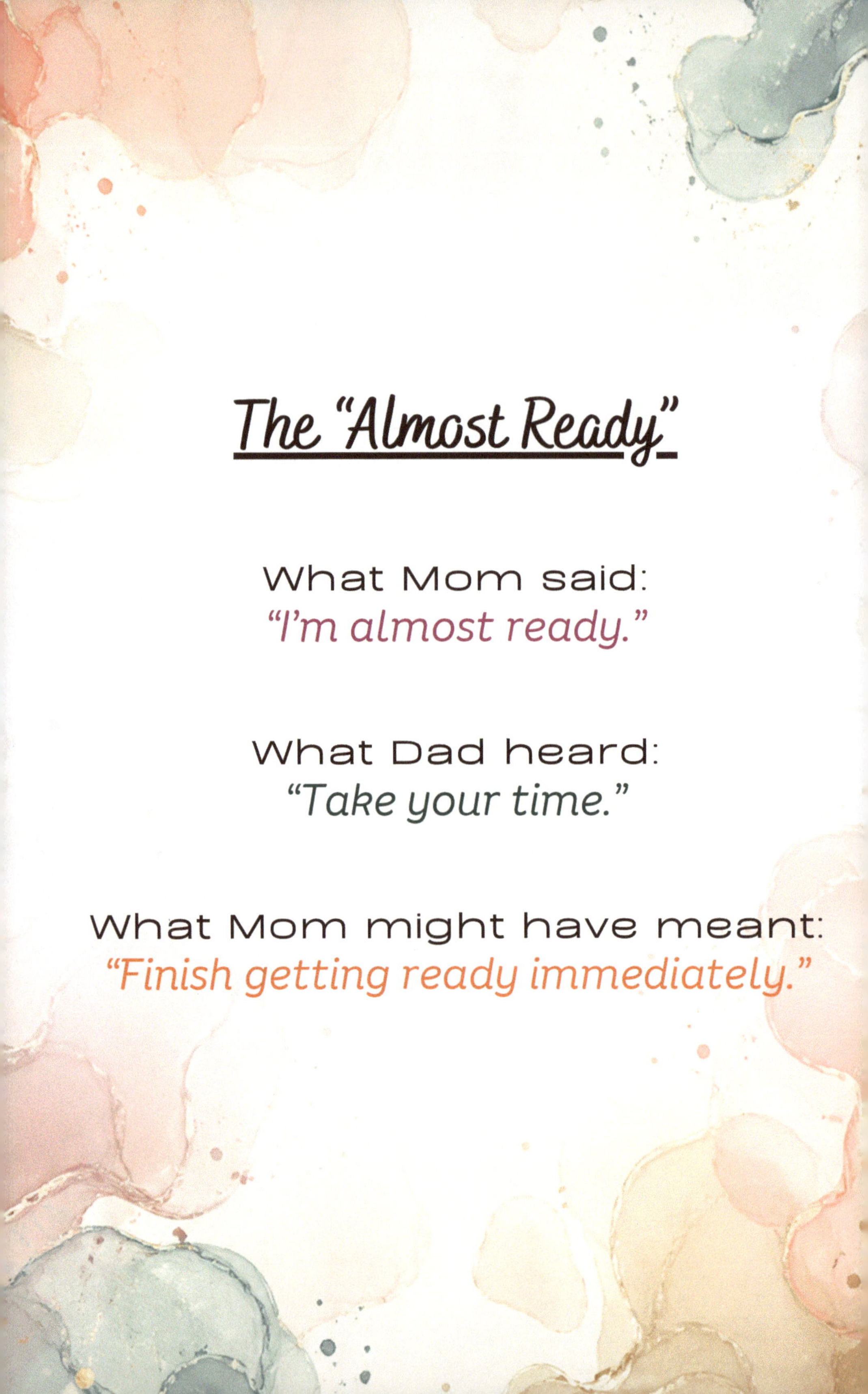

## The "Almost Ready"

What Mom said:
*"I'm almost ready."*

What Dad heard:
*"Take your time."*

What Mom might have meant:
*"Finish getting ready immediately."*

HOME
SWEET
HOME

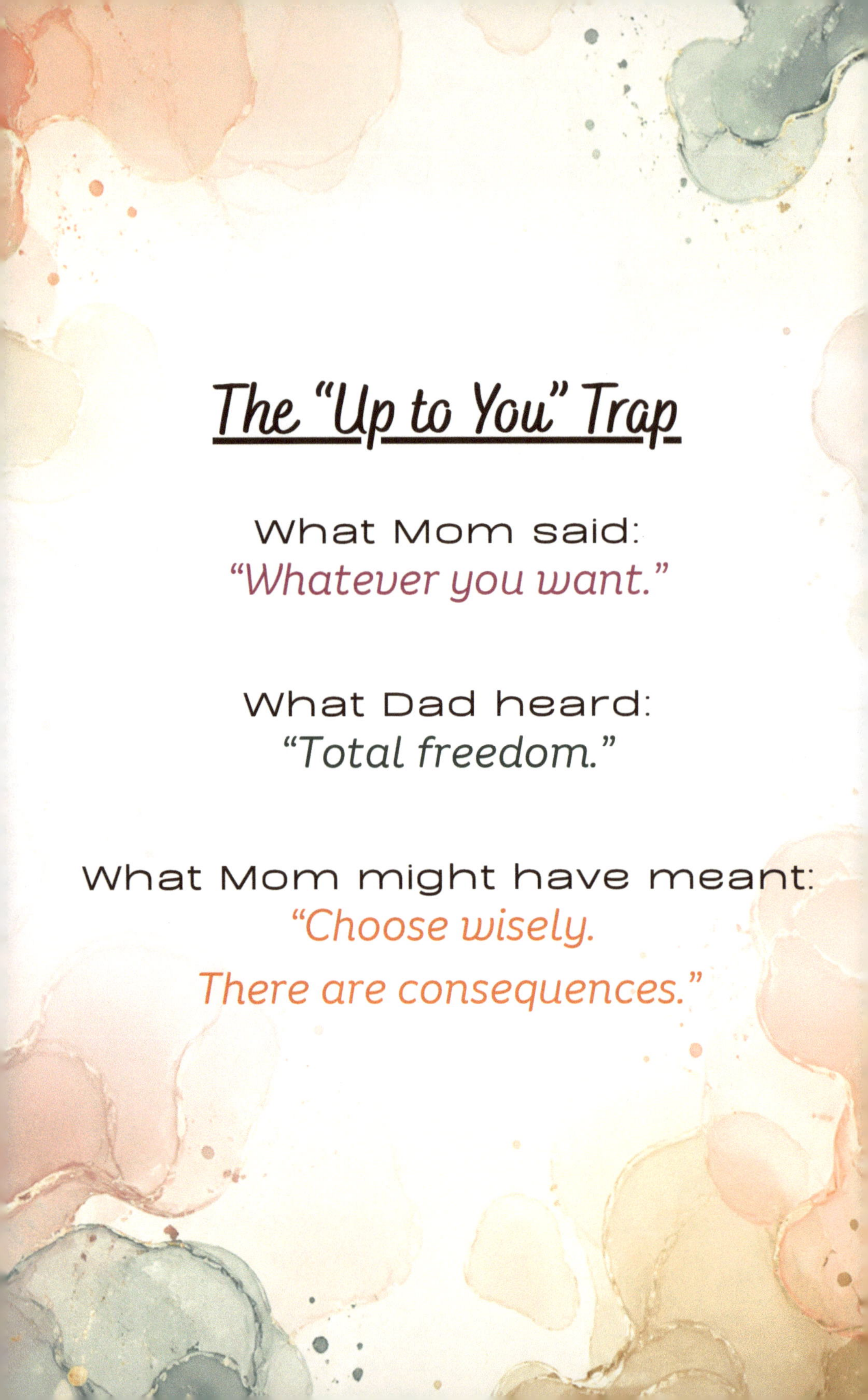

# The "Up to You" Trap

What Mom said:

*"Whatever you want."*

What Dad heard:

*"Total freedom."*

What Mom might have meant:

*"Choose wisely.*

*There are consequences."*

COCOA PEBBLES
Reese's Puffs
Lucky Charms
Takis
nutella
OREO
Cheetos
Lay's
Classic
Skittles
OREO

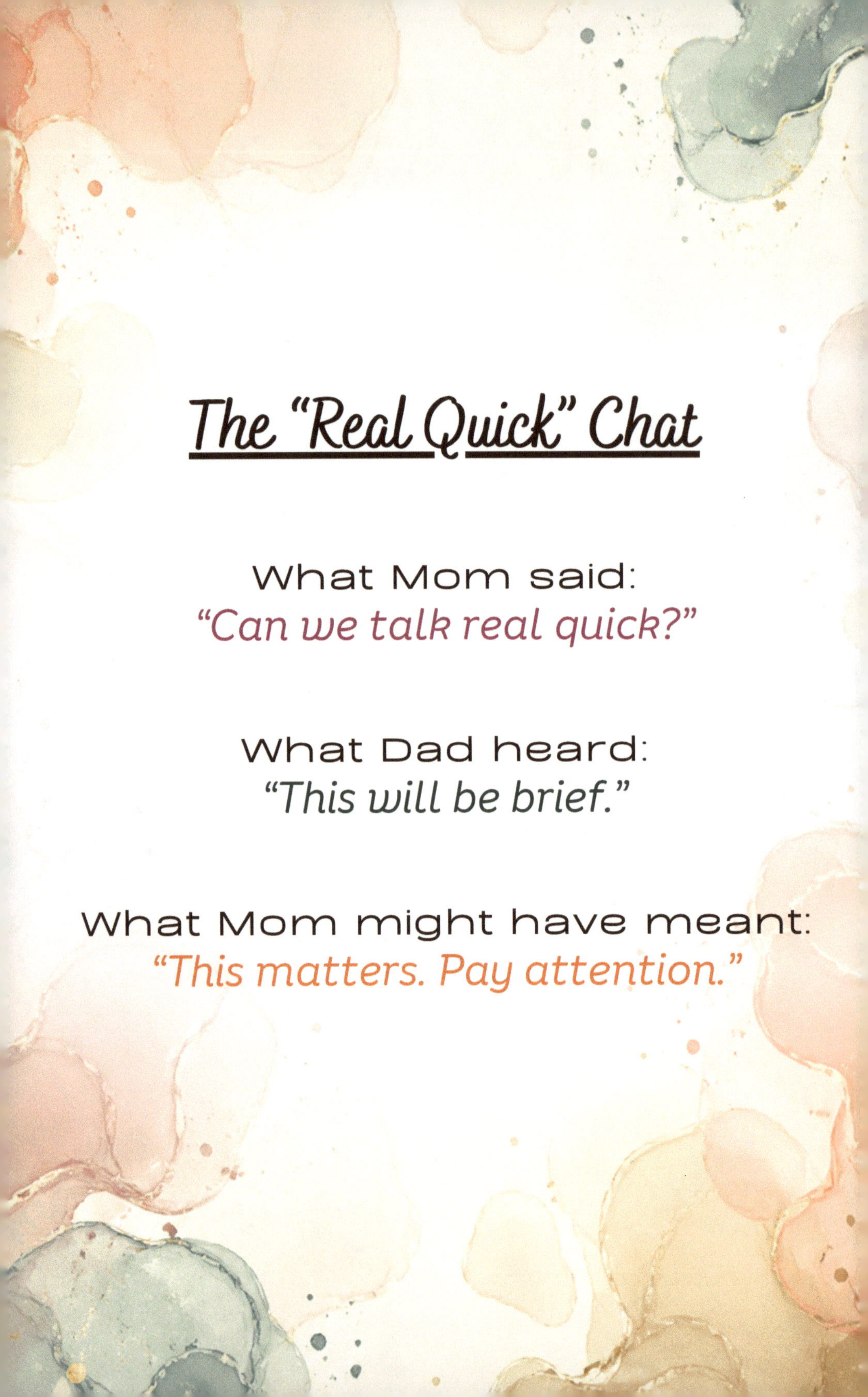

# The "Real Quick" Chat

What Mom said:

*"Can we talk real quick?"*

What Dad heard:

*"This will be brief."*

What Mom might have meant:

*"This matters. Pay attention."*

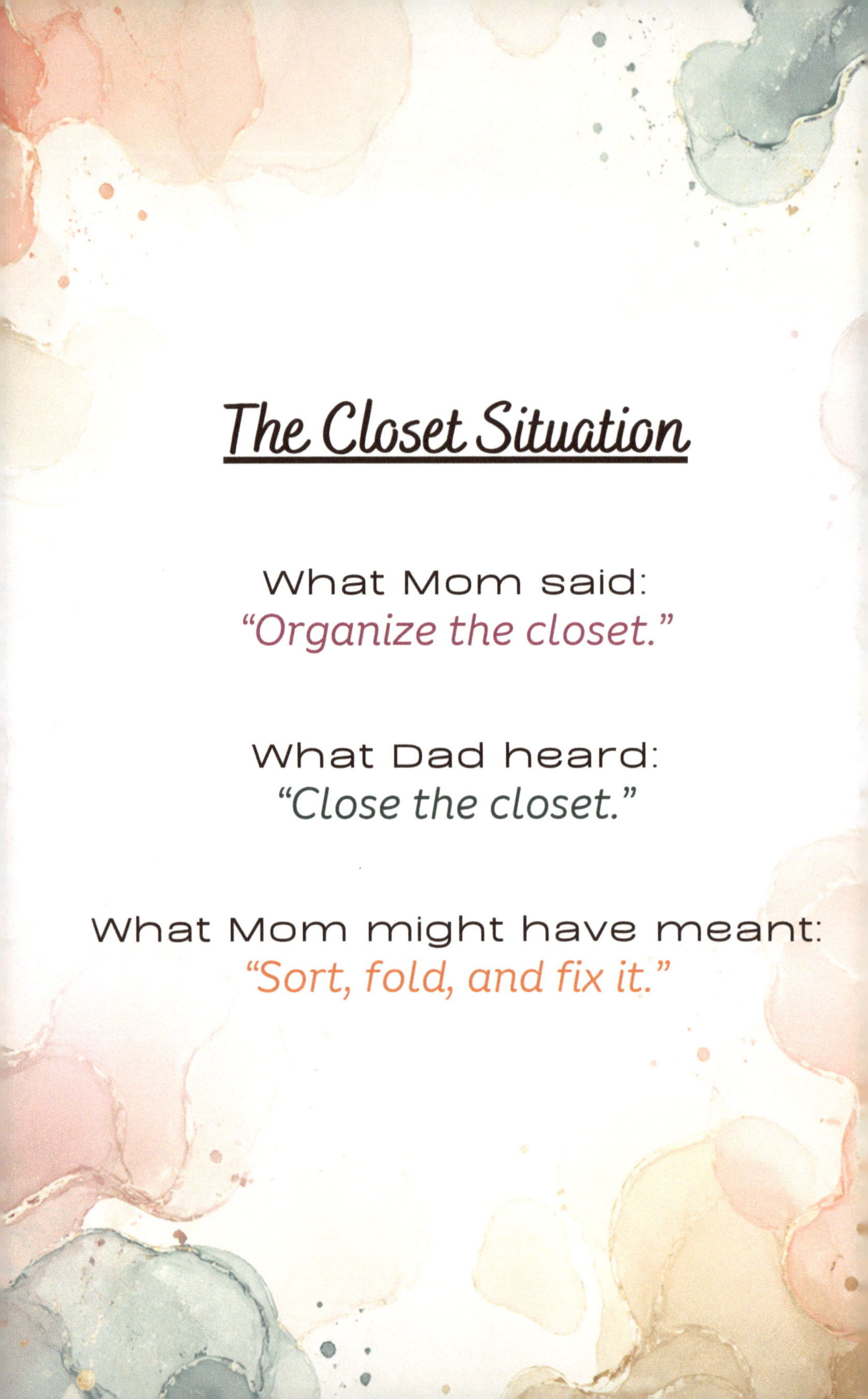

# The Closet Situation

What Mom said:
*"Organize the closet."*

What Dad heard:
*"Close the closet."*

What Mom might have meant:
*"Sort, fold, and fix it."*

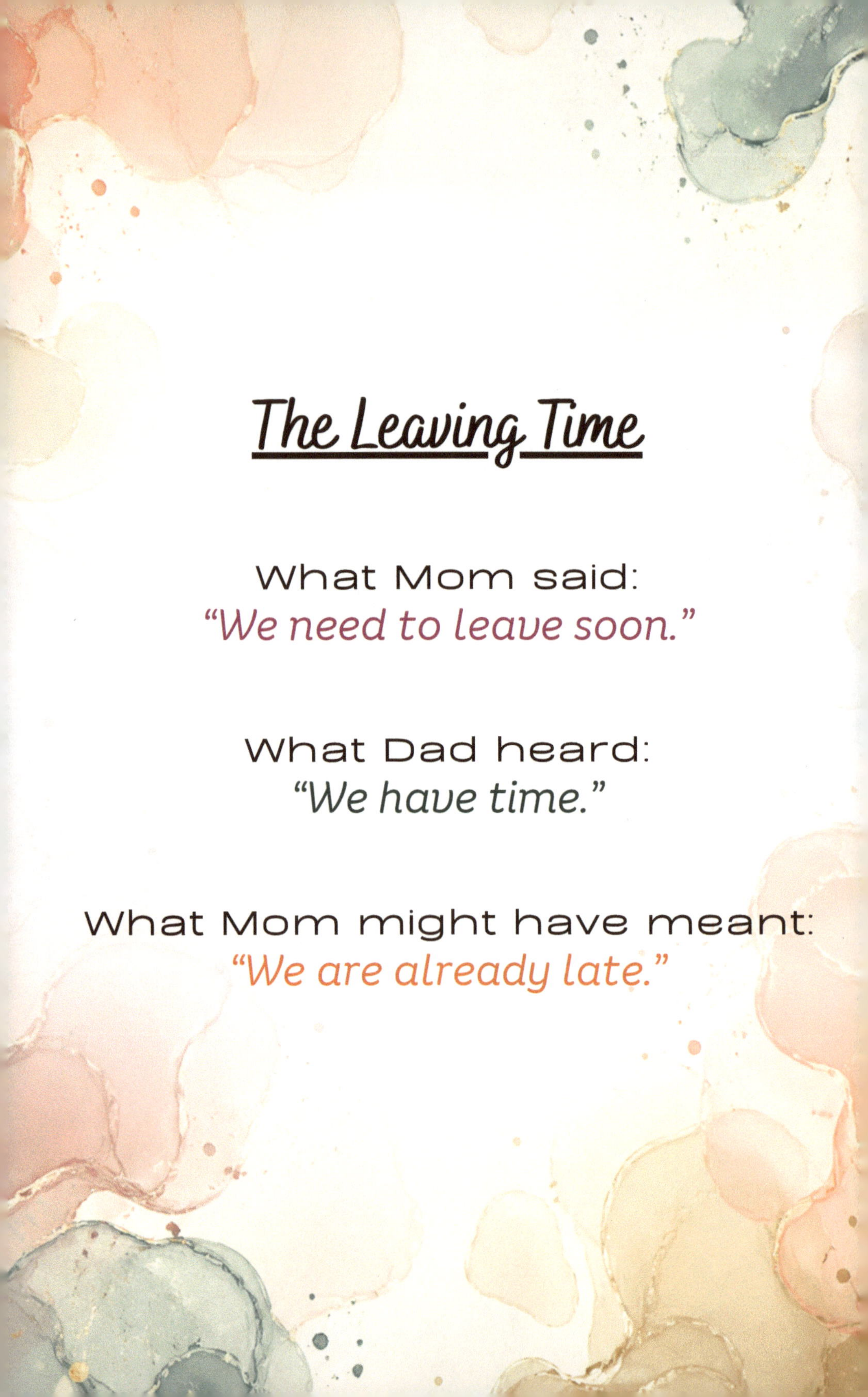

# The Leaving Time

What Mom said:
*"We need to leave soon."*

What Dad heard:
*"We have time."*

What Mom might have meant:
*"We are already late."*

Don't
forget!

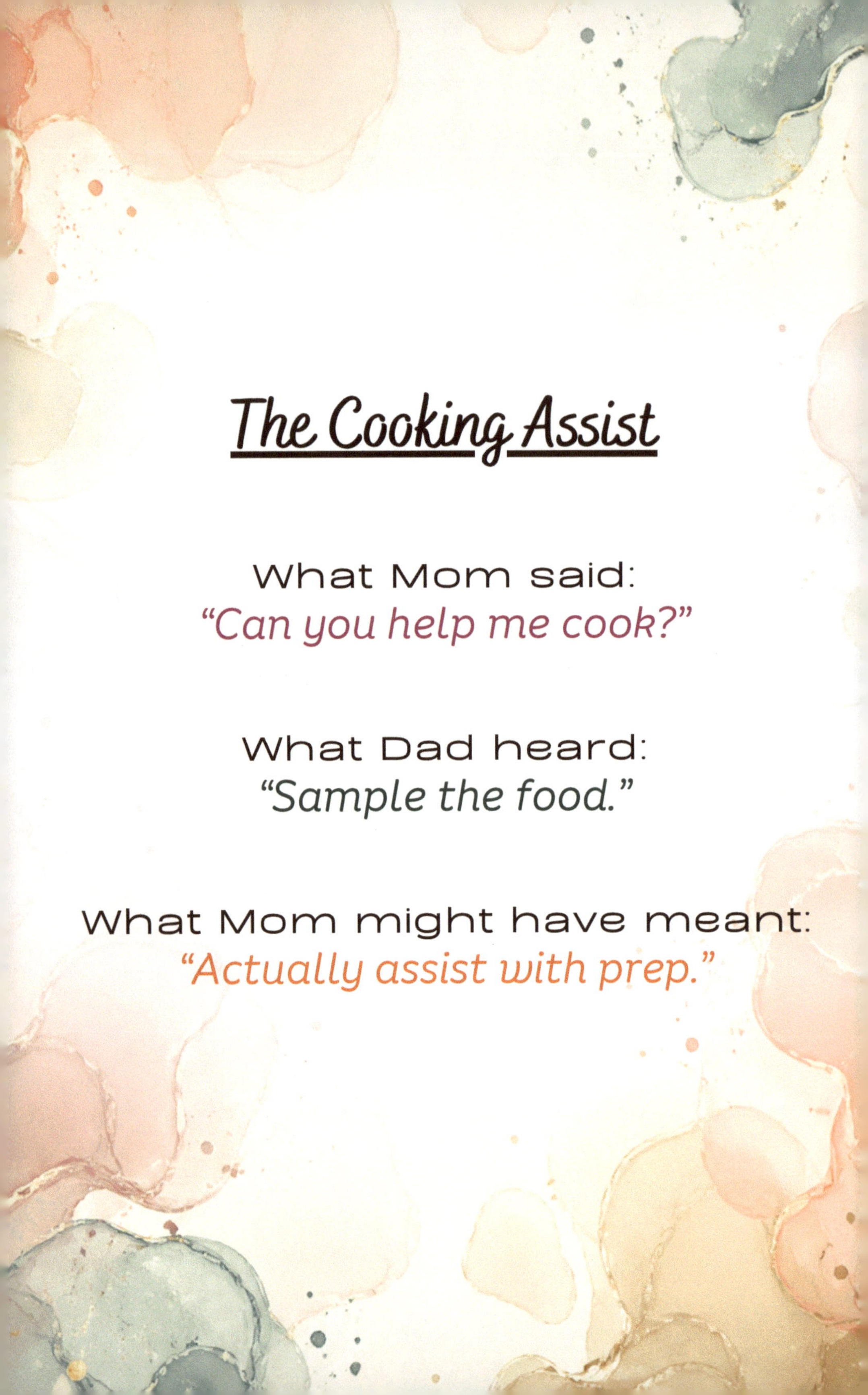

# The Cooking Assist

What Mom said:
*"Can you help me cook?"*

What Dad heard:
*"Sample the food."*

What Mom might have meant:
*"Actually assist with prep."*

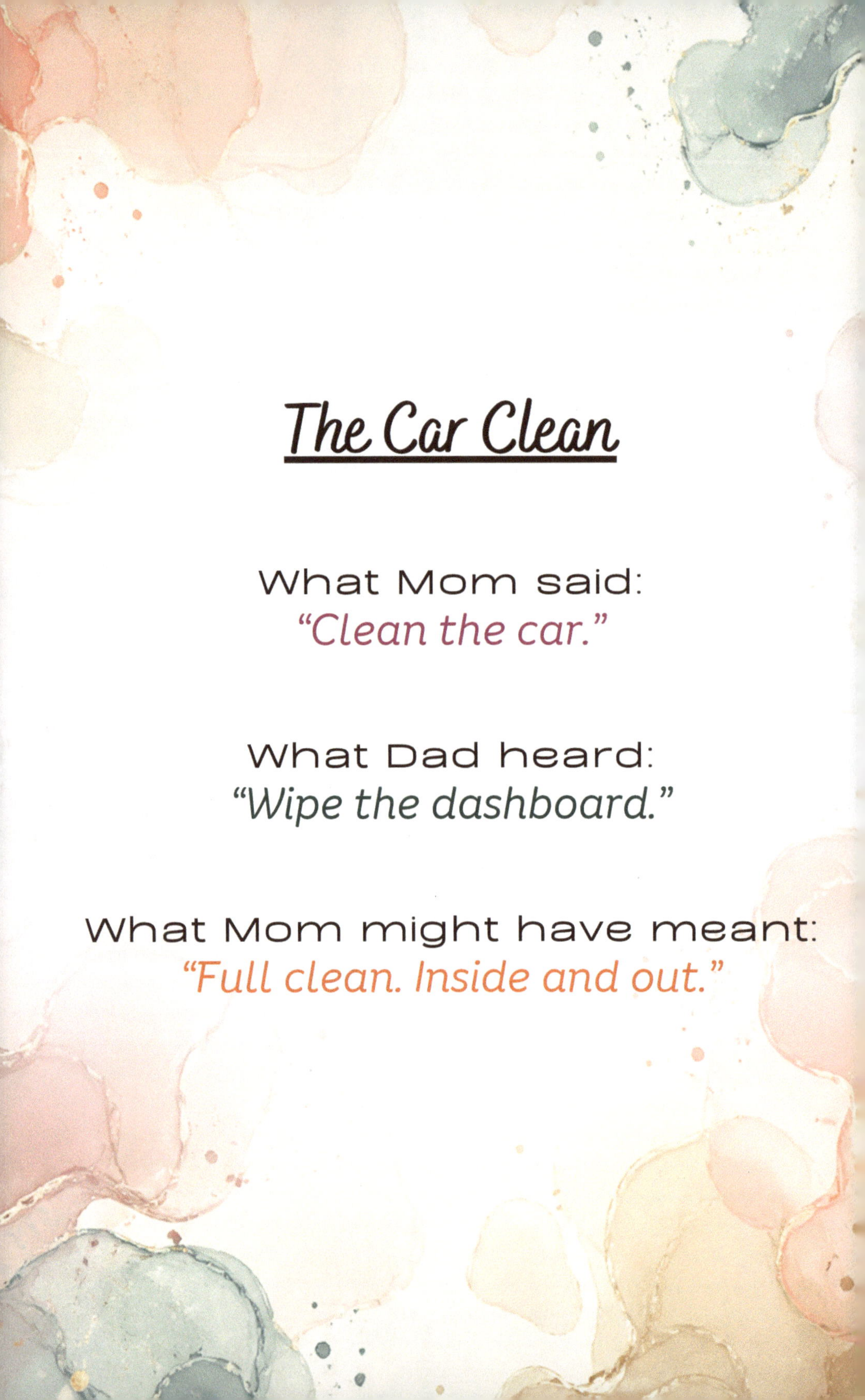

# The Car Clean

What Mom said:
*"Clean the car."*

What Dad heard:
*"Wipe the dashboard."*

What Mom might have meant:
*"Full clean. Inside and out."*

# The Kid Volume

What Mom said:
*"They're being loud."*

What Dad heard:
*"They're having fun."*

What Mom might have meant:
*"Please intervene."*

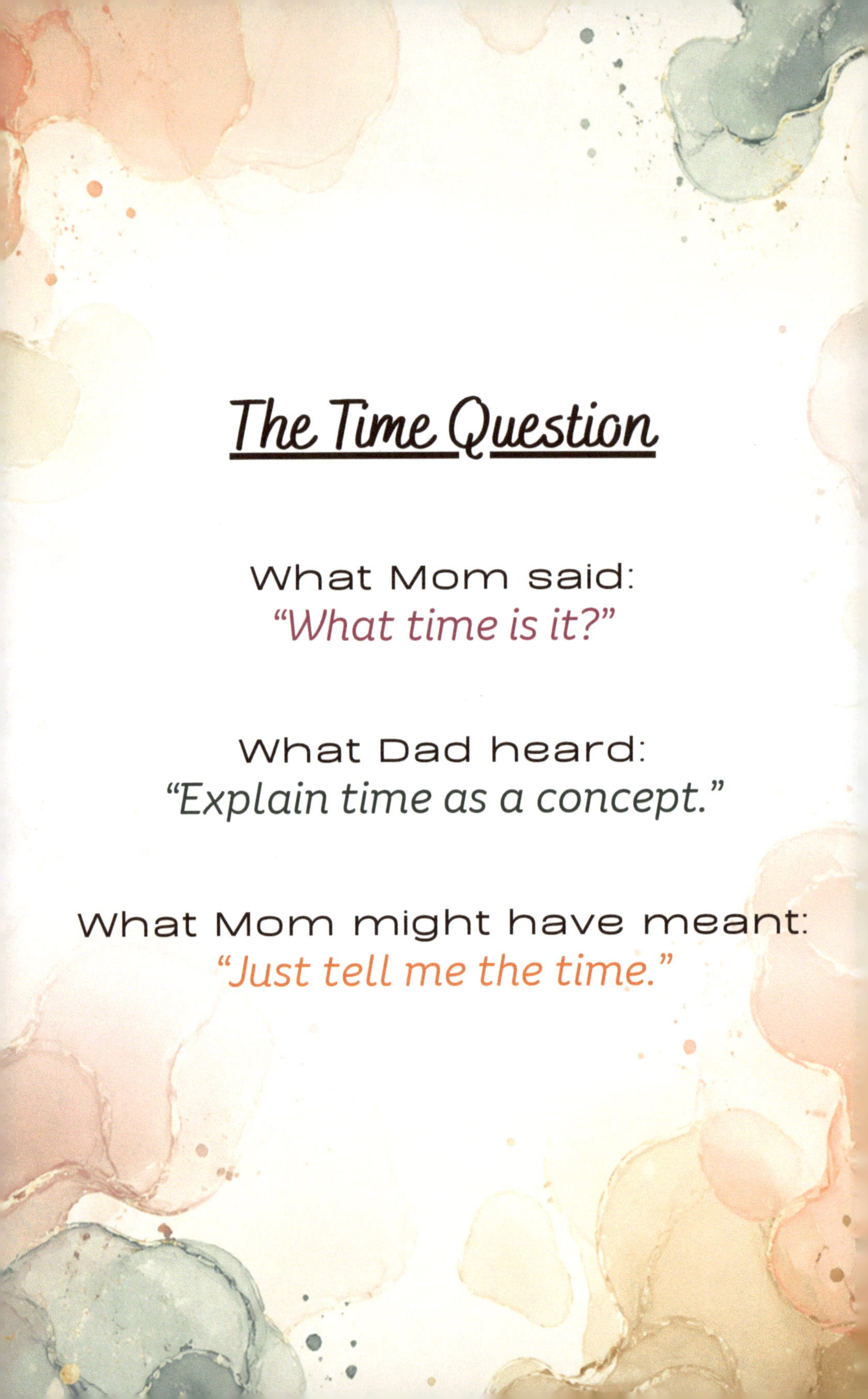

# The Time Question

What Mom said:
*"What time is it?"*

What Dad heard:
*"Explain time as a concept."*

What Mom might have meant:
*"Just tell me the time."*

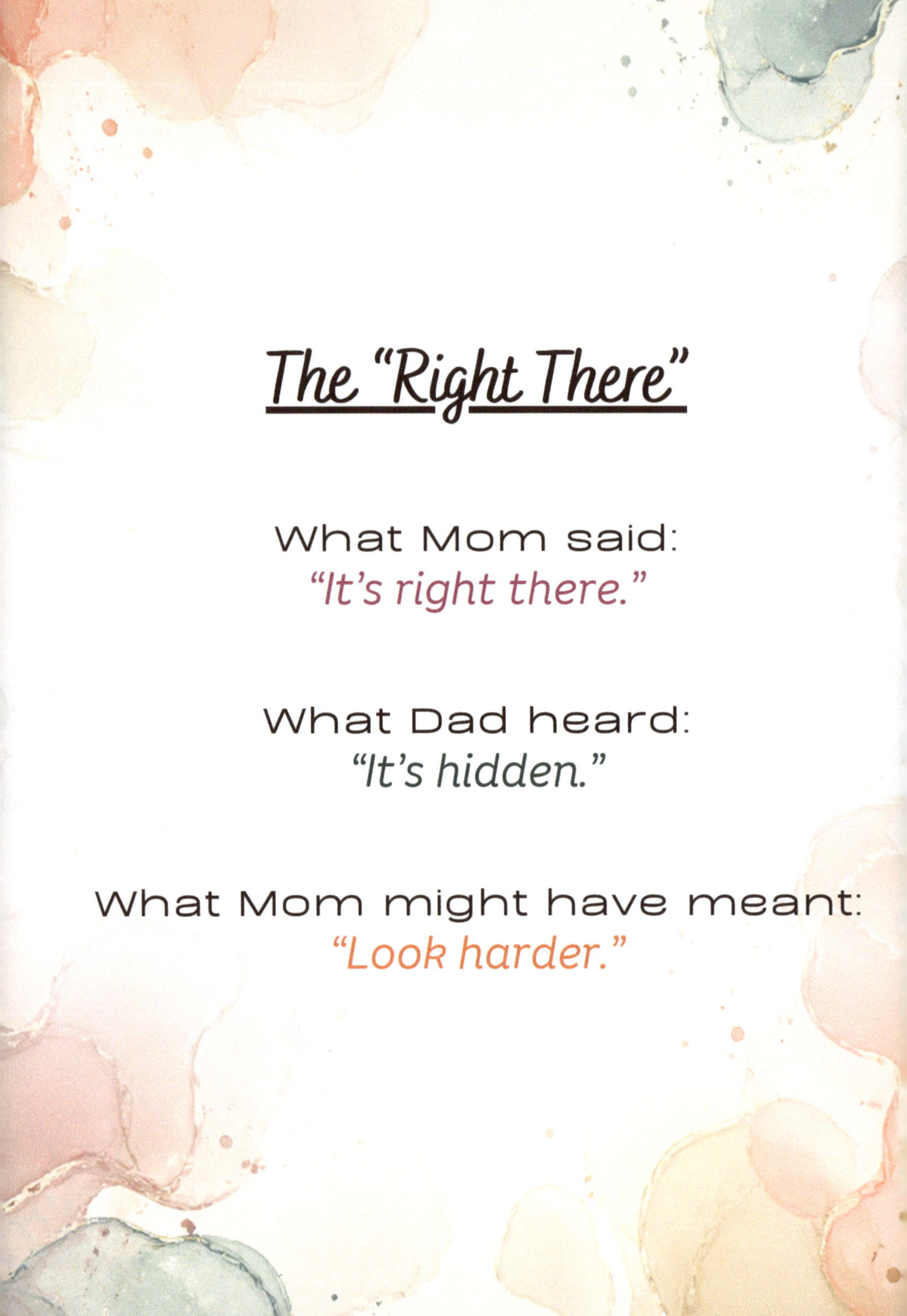

## The "Right There"

What Mom said:
*"It's right there."*

What Dad heard:
*"It's hidden."*

What Mom might have meant:
*"Look harder."*

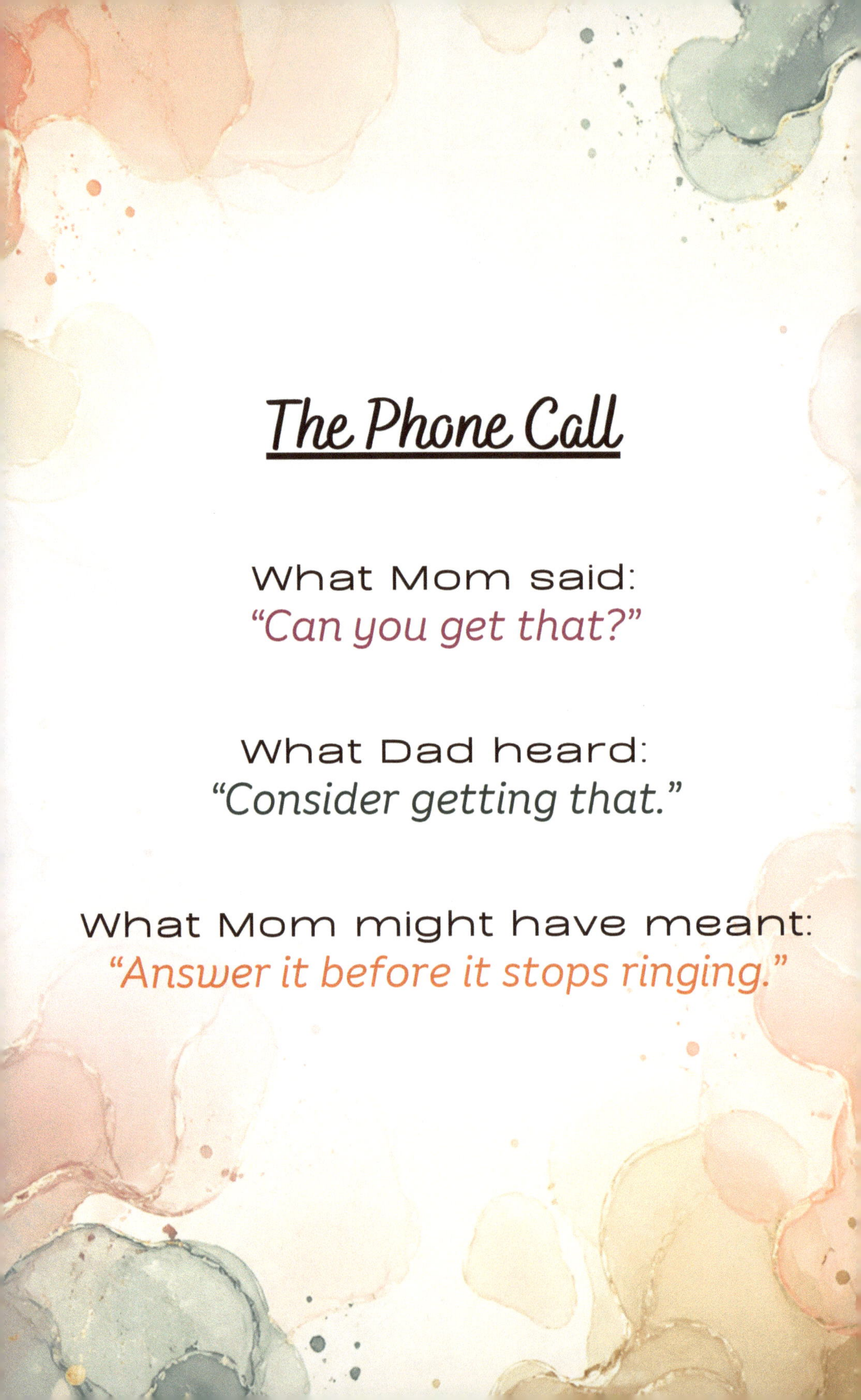

# The Phone Call

What Mom said:
*"Can you get that?"*

What Dad heard:
*"Consider getting that."*

What Mom might have meant:
*"Answer it before it stops ringing."*

HOME
Sweet
HOME

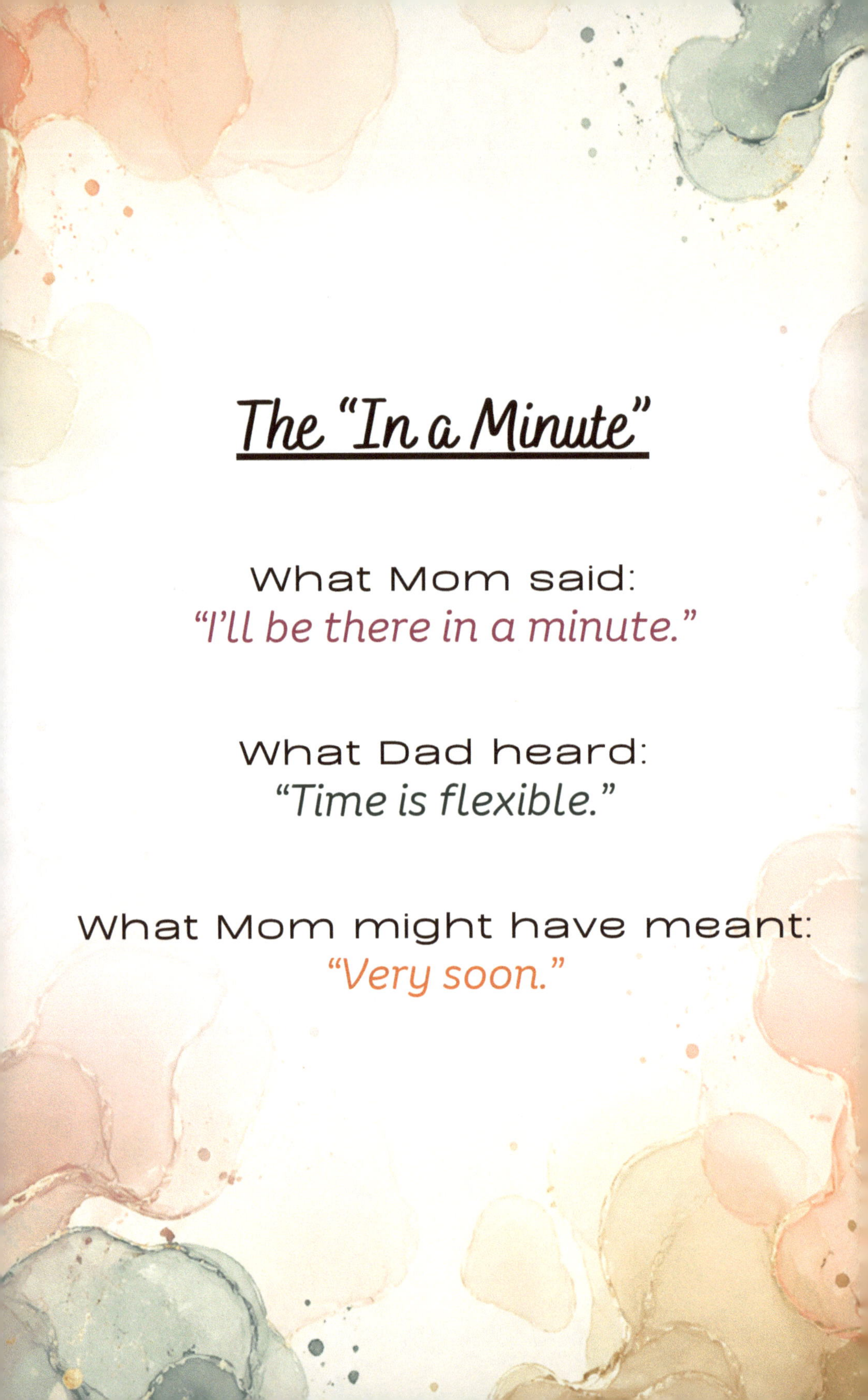

## The "In a Minute"

What Mom said:
*"I'll be there in a minute."*

What Dad heard:
*"Time is flexible."*

What Mom might have meant:
*"Very soon."*

# The Packing Situation

What Mom said:

*"Help pack."*

What Dad heard:

*"Throw items into a bag with confidence."*

What Mom might have meant:

*"Pack logically."*

10:47

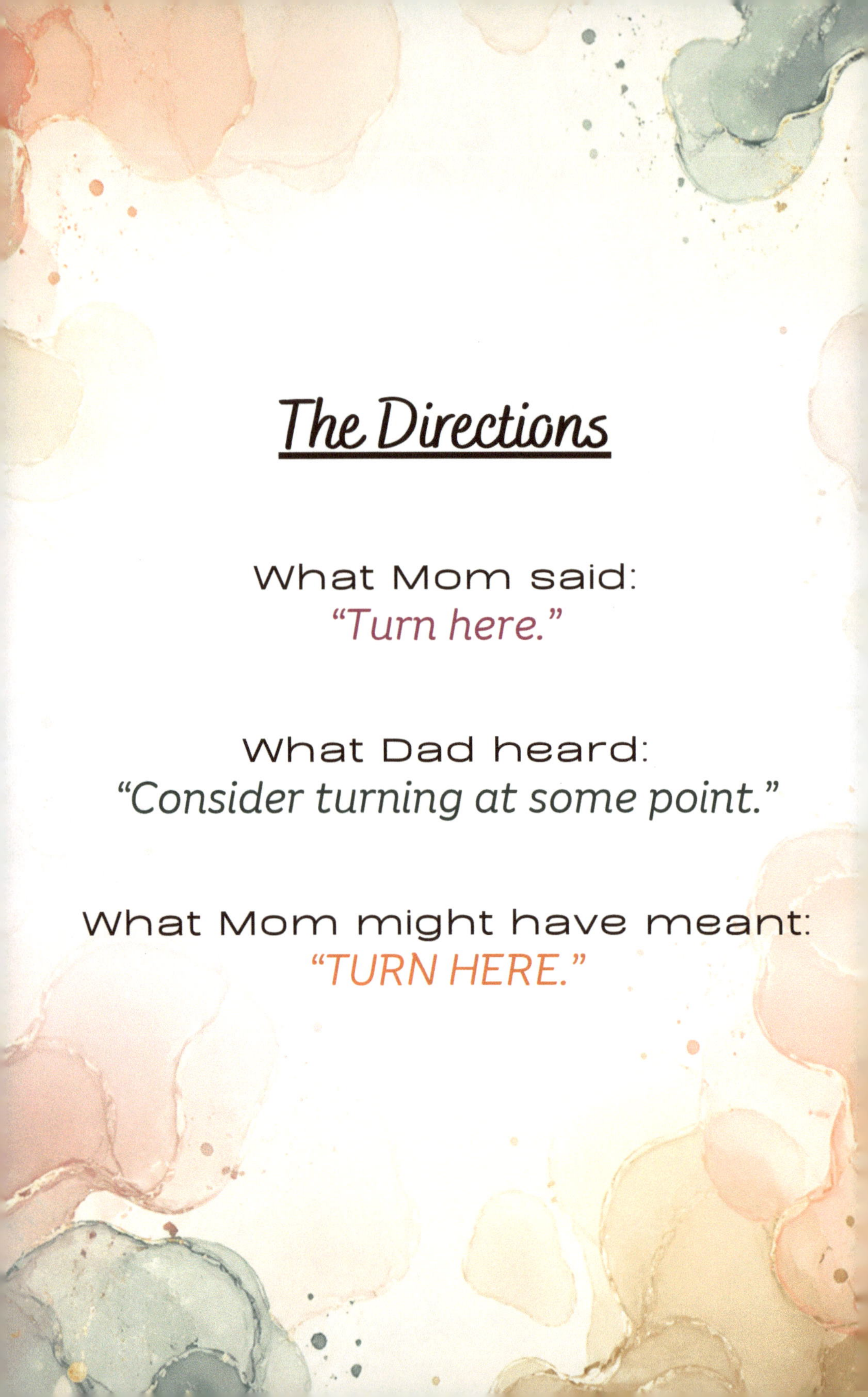

# The Directions

What Mom said:

*"Turn here."*

What Dad heard:

*"Consider turning at some point."*

What Mom might have meant:

*"TURN HERE."*

WRONG
WAY

## The "Hold This" Moment

What Mom said:
*"Can you hold this?"*

What Dad heard:
*"Take one item and freeze."*

What Mom might have meant:
*"Please take several things so I can function again."*

What Mom said:
*"How does this look?"*

What Dad heard:
*"Say it looks good immediately."*

What Mom might have meant:
*"Actually look.*
*With your eyes."*

What Mom said:
*"Do you mind doing this?"*

What Dad heard:
*"This is optional."*

What Mom might have meant:
*"Yes, I mind. Please do it."*

WASH
DRY
FOLD
REPEAT

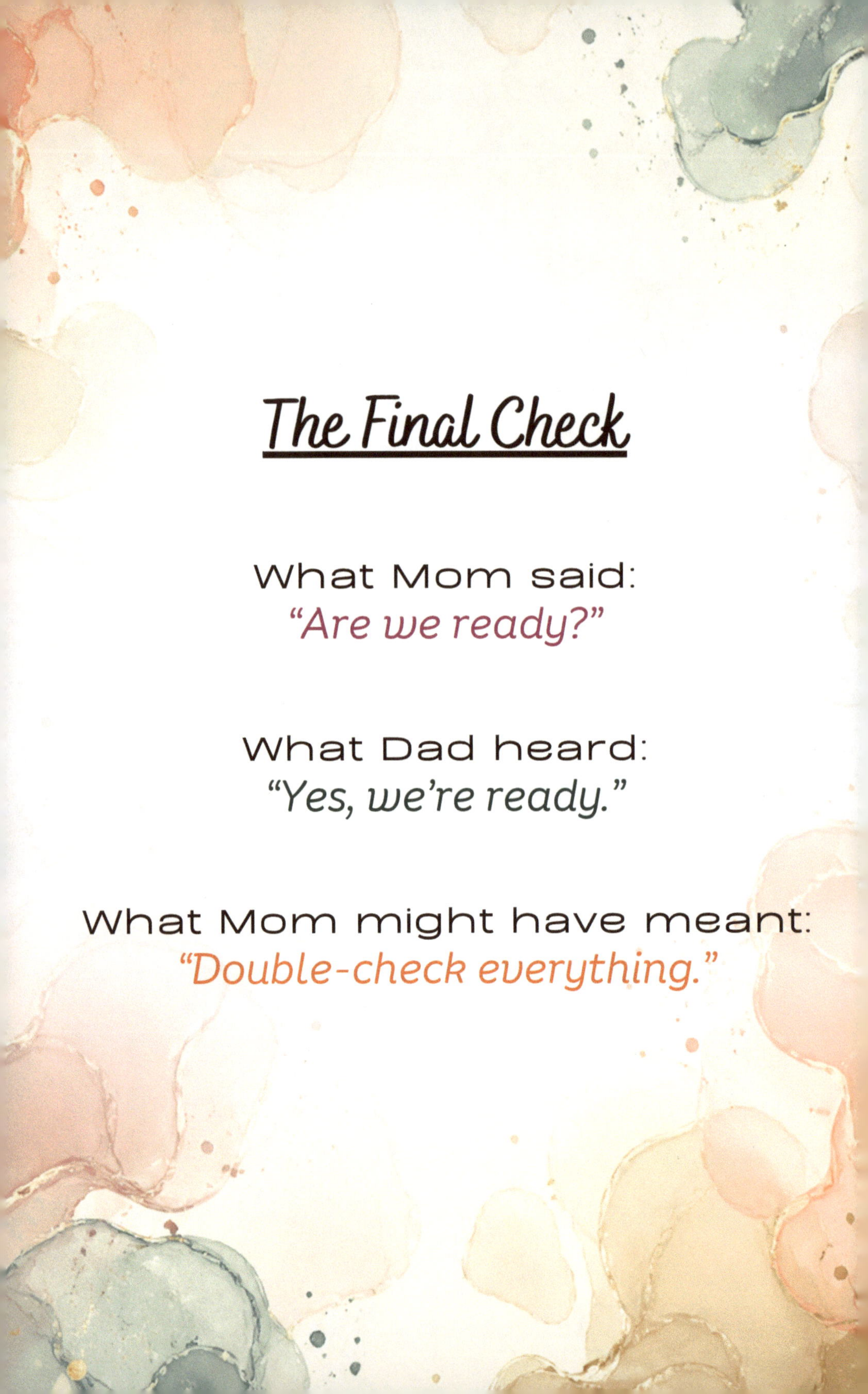

# The Final Check

What Mom said:
*"Are we ready?"*

What Dad heard:
*"Yes, we're ready."*

What Mom might have meant:
*"Double-check everything."*

And just like that, the conversations keep going.

Some land perfectly.
Some take a scenic route.
And some... become stories you'll laugh about later.

Because in the middle of the mix-ups, the half-heard moments, and the "that's not what I meant," there's something bigger holding it all together.

We're still showing up.
Still trying.
Still figuring each other out, one conversation at a time.

And somehow... that's more than enough.

Hello, there!

In every conversation, there's a moment—small and easy to miss—where understanding has a chance to grow.

Sometimes we get it right.
Sometimes we don't.

But what matters most is that we keep trying. We keep choosing to listen a little closer, speak a little clearer, and meet each other with a little more patience than before.

Because connection isn't built on perfect words.
It's built on effort. On grace. On showing up again, even after something gets lost along the way.

So if you've ever felt misunderstood, or realized you may have missed something too, take heart in this:

You're learning. You're growing. You're doing better than you think.

And every time you try again, you're building something stronger than perfect communication—you're building understanding.

With Googolplex Love,

MommyHooray

# What Was Said vs. What Was Heard

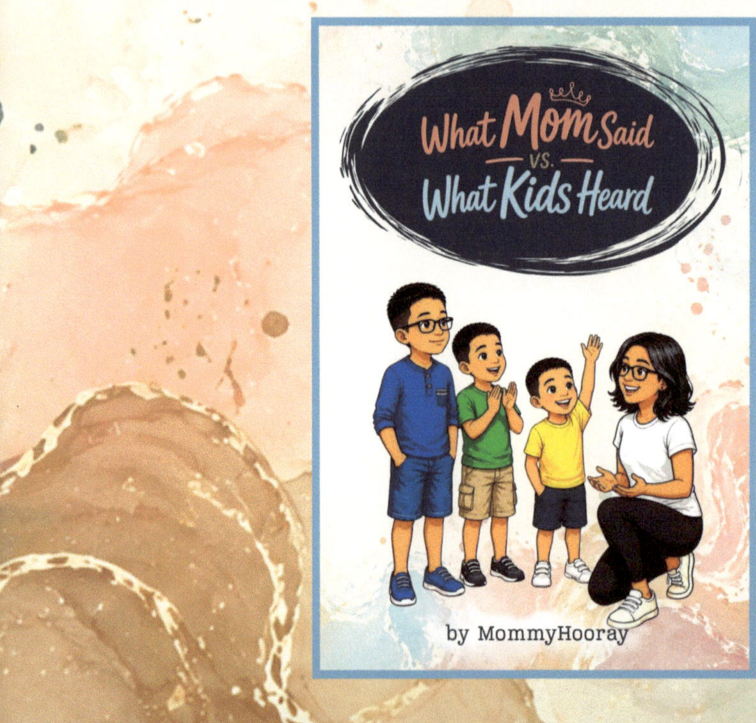

# Also by MommyHooray

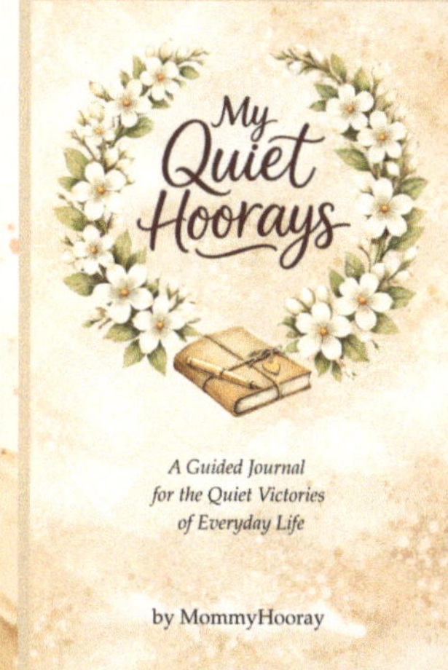


**... and more!**

# From My Heart to Yours

*Write something meaningful*
*for the person who will cherish this book, or for yourself.*

Today's Date: ________________

*May this page find you again, years from now.*

www.ingramcontent.com/pod-product-compliance
Lightning Source LLC
LaVergne TN
LVHW052256100826
845147LV00001B/66

*9781972071571*